I0815548

EVERYTHING ✕ SPORTS
EVERYTHING
MLB
BY DONNA McKINNEY
eureka!

Eureka! books turn real stories into unforgettable experiences. This nonfiction imprint sparks curiosity, encourages critical thinking, and engages middle-grade readers. *Eureka!* books empower young minds to explore the stories of the real world, one fascinating fact at a time. Unravel the power of knowledge and lifelong learning with *Eureka!*

This edition first published in 2026 by Bellwether Media, Inc.

Library of Congress Cataloging-in-Publication Data

Names: McKinney, Donna B. (Donna Bowen) author
Title: Everything MLB / by Donna McKinney. Other titles: Everything Major League Baseball
Description: Minneapolis, MN : Bellwether Media, Inc., 2026. | Series: Everything sports | "Eureka!"--Cover page 1 | Audience: Ages 9-15 | Audience: Grades 7-9 | Summary: "Engaging images accompany information on MLB. The text level and subject matter are intended for students in grades 5 through 9"-- Provided by publisher.
Identifiers: LCCN 2025020008 (print) | LCCN 2025020009 (ebook) | ISBN 9798893045581 library binding | ISBN 9798893046960 ebook
Subjects: LCSH: Major League Baseball (Organization) | Baseball--United States--Management | Baseball--Economic aspects--United States | Baseball fans--United States
Classification: LCC GV875.A1 M345 2026 (print) | LCC GV875.A1 (ebook) | DDC 796.357/64--dc23/eng/20250621
LC record available at https://lccn.loc.gov/2025020008
LC ebook record available at https://lccn.loc.gov/2025020009

Editor: Kieran Downs Designer: Jeffrey Kollock

Printed in the United States of America, North Mankato, MN.

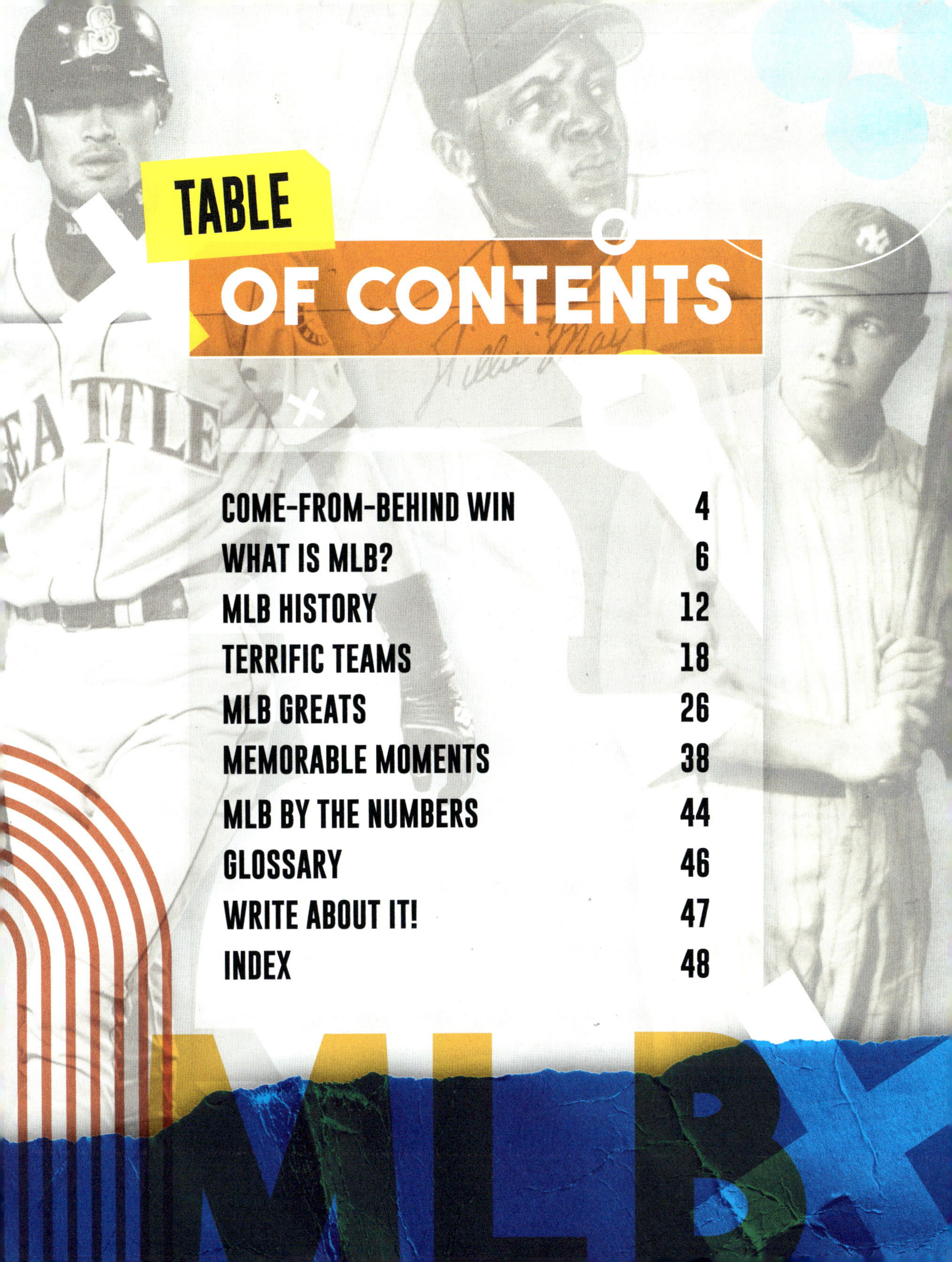

TABLE OF CONTENTS

COME-FROM-BEHIND WIN

It is the 2023 World Series. The Texas Rangers and Arizona Diamondbacks are playing. This is the first game of the best-of-seven series. Heading into the ninth inning, the Diamondbacks lead 5–3. It looks like the Diamondbacks might be heading to victory. Then, with a runner on base, Rangers shortstop Corey Seager hits a home run that ties the game. They are headed to extra innings.

Through the 10th inning, neither team scores. In the bottom of the 11th inning, with one out, Rangers right fielder Adolis García comes to bat. García's bat smacks the ball hard. Fans erupt in wild cheers as the ball clears the right field wall. It is a **walk-off** home run! García raises his arm in celebration and trots around the bases. His cheering teammates wait for him at home plate. The Rangers come from behind to win the game 6–5!

COREY SEAGER'S HOME RUN

RANGERS WIN THE SERIES

The Rangers won the 2023 World Series in five games. It was the first time the team won a World Series.

ADOLIS GARCÍA'S HOME RUN
Globe Life Field
FOX
WORLD SERIES
BEASLEY
27
53

WHAT IS MLB?

Major League Baseball (MLB) is a professional baseball league in North America. There are 30 teams in MLB. These teams are located in cities in the United States and Canada. The 30 teams are divided into the **American League** (AL) and the **National League** (NL). The teams are arranged into six **divisions**. Each league has three divisions.

Teams usually play series of two to four games against the same opponent. These series take place on **consecutive** days in the same ballpark. Teams play games at home with a visiting team coming to their ballpark. Later in the season, they will play another series against the same team at the other team's ballpark. When a team travels to play in other ballparks, it is called a road trip.

MINOR LEAGUE LEVELS

There are different levels of minor league teams. These are Rookie Ball, Low-A, High-A, Double-A, and Triple-A. Triple-A teams are the highest level of minor league teams.

MLB TEAMS

AMERICAN LEAGUE

AL East

AL West

AL Central

NATIONAL LEAGUE

NL East

NL West

NL Central

MINOR LEAGUE GAME

Every MLB team has **minor league** teams that belong to them. These teams are called their **farm system**. Players coming out of high school or college often play for minor league teams before moving up to an MLB team. These minor league teams are usually located in smaller towns away from the home city of their MLB team.

The MLB **preseason** starts in February with Spring Training. All MLB teams have a training camp in either Florida or Arizona. Teams train and play practice games against each other during Spring Training. The teams training in Florida play games against each other in the Grapefruit League. The teams training in Arizona play each other in the Cactus League. These preseason games do not count for a team's regular season record.

The MLB regular season starts in late March or early April and lasts about six months. Teams play 162 games in the MLB regular season. It is the most games played in any regular season of any professional sport. Each team plays many games against the teams in their own division. They also play some games against teams in other divisions and the other league. Each MLB team plays all the other MLB teams during the regular season.

The MLB **draft** takes place every July. The draft lasts several days. Teams choose from the best players coming out of high school and college. Teams with the worst records the previous season have the first choices in the draft.

SPRING TRAINING GAME

MLB AWARDS

CY YOUNG

Two awards given each year to the best pitcher in each league

2024 MLB DRAFT

FREE AGENTS

A free agent is a player who can sign a contract with any MLB team. Players become free agents when they have played in MLB for six years or are released by their team.

GOLDEN GLOVE

Award given to the best defensive player at each position in each league

MOST VALUABLE PLAYER

Award given to the player in each league who had the best season

2024 HALL OF FAME INDUCTEES

HALL OF FAME

The National Baseball Hall of Fame and Museum is located in Cooperstown, New York. Each year a few players are elected to the Hall of Fame. American baseball writers vote for the players to be added.

PLAYOFF GAME

WORLD SERIES

After the season, teams play in **playoff** games. The 12 best teams play each other for a chance to compete in the World Series. These playoff games are split between the AL and NL. The six teams that win each of the MLB divisions automatically make the playoffs. Six more teams, three from each league, are also in the playoffs. These six teams are **Wild Card** teams. These teams have the best records behind the teams that won each division.

The playoffs begin with the Wild Card Series. Teams play each other in a best-of-three series. Teams that win the Wild Card Series move on to the Division Series. They play against the two division winners with the best records. They play a best-of-five series. The winners of the Division Series then face each other in the League Championship Series. This is a best-of-seven series. The two League Championship winners play each other in the World Series in a best-of-seven format. The World Series winner is the MLB champion.

MLB gives Most Valuable Player (MVP) awards to the best player in the AL and NL each year. Sportswriters who cover baseball news vote for these two awards. The winners are announced after the World Series.

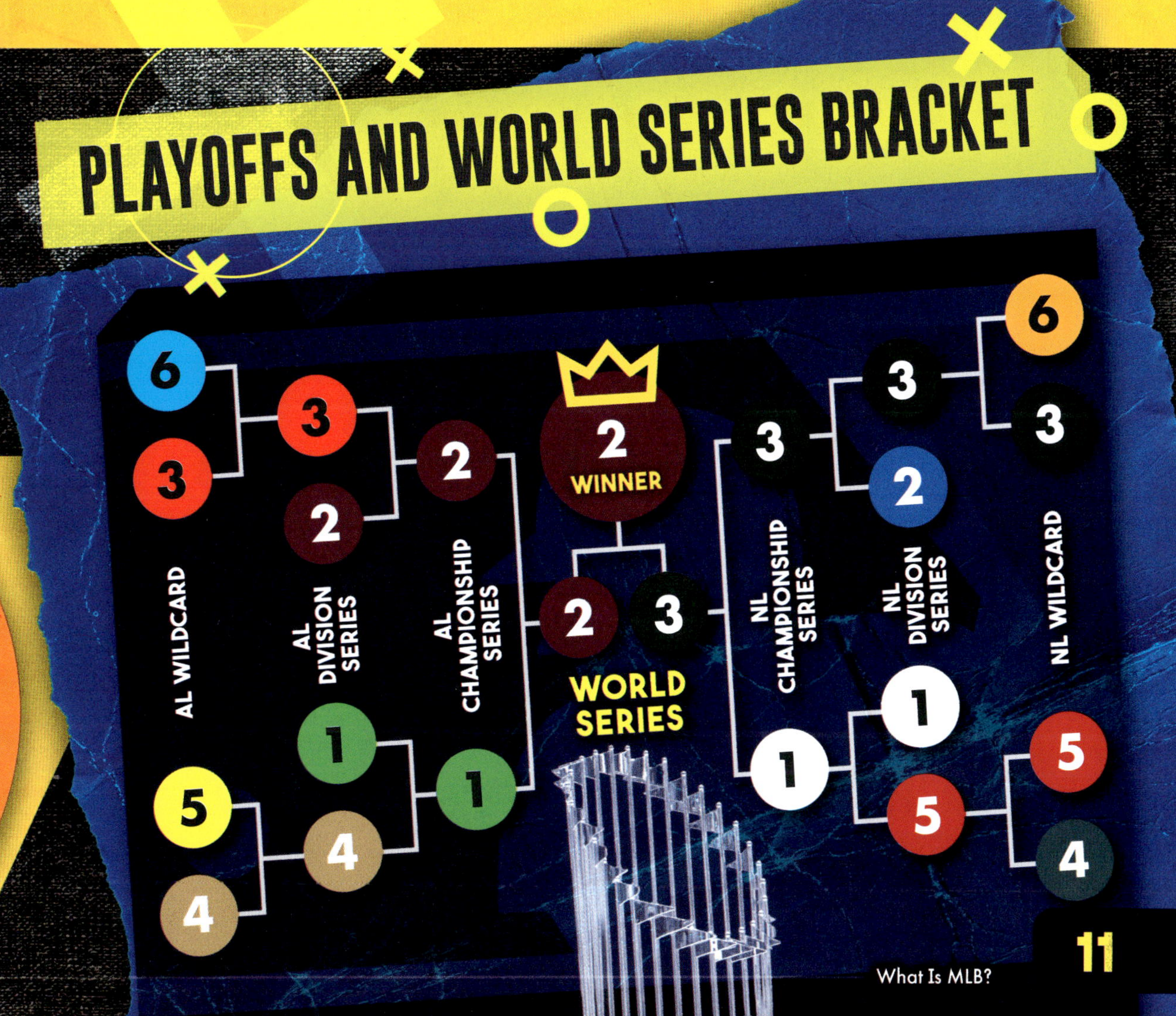

MLB HISTORY

Baseball started in the United States in the mid-1800s. It began as a pickup game played for fun and then grew into an organized sport with several different leagues. The NL started in the late 1800s. The AL formed in 1901. The NL and AL competed for the best players and fans.

MLB was born in 1903 when the NL and AL joined to form a single league. When the two leagues joined, both leagues had eight teams each. The teams played a 140-game schedule. That year, the two leagues held the first World Series. The best team from each league played to decide a national champion. It was a best-of-nine-game series. The World Series changed between a best-of-seven format and best-of-nine format for many years. In 1922, the league decided to keep the best-of-seven format.

When the two leagues joined, a group called the National Commission was formed to lead MLB. This group of three people led MLB for many years. In 1921, baseball began to be led by a single **commissioner**. The commissioner directs the business of the league. MLB is still run by a commissioner today.

FIRST WORLD SERIES

In 1903, the Boston Americans and the Pittsburgh Pirates played the first official World Series. Boston won five games to three.

FIRST MLB COMMISSIONER, KENESAW MOUNTAIN LANDIS

In the early years, baseball was only played during the day. The first night game played under lights happened in 1935 at the home of the Cincinnati Reds in Cincinnati, Ohio. Soon more and more MLB Stadiums added lights and night games. Before 1947, MLB was **segregated**. Black players were not allowed to play. That changed when Jackie Robinson took the field for the Brooklyn Dodgers on April 15, 1947. Many more Black players would join the league in the following years.

FIRST NIGHT GAME, 1935

1961 MLB GAME

In 1961, MLB began to expand. The years since 1961 are called the Expansion Era in baseball. As teams were added, other changes also happened. When expansion began, MLB shifted to a 162-game schedule. MLB also added more **postseason** games. Over the course of the 1960s, eight teams were added.

In 1973, the AL added the designated hitter rule. This let teams use another player to bat in place of their pitcher. In 1977, the AL added two more teams. In 1993, the NL added two more teams. This brought the total number of MLB teams to 28.

FLORIDA MARLINS, ADDED TO THE NL IN 1993

LAST TO LIGHT

Wrigley Field, home of the Chicago Cubs, was the last MLB stadium to install lights. The stadium installed the lights in 1988.

1997 INTERLEAGUE PLAY

2013 HOUSTON ASTROS GAME

Interleague play came to MLB in 1997. Before that time, AL teams and NL teams only played each other during Spring Training and in the World Series. Interleague games happened only a few times during the season. The games all took place in the early part of the season. In 1998, both the AL and NL added a team. This brought the total number of MLB teams to 30.

In 2013, the Houston Astros moved from the NL to the AL. The move brought balance to the two leagues. With the Astros in the AL, both leagues had three divisions with five teams in each division. Interleague play expanded to happen throughout the whole regular season. MLB also expanded the playoffs in 2013, adding two more Wild Card teams to the playoff schedule. In 2022, MLB adopted the universal designated hitter rule. This brought the designated hitter to the NL. That same year, MLB expanded the playoff schedule by adding a third Wild Card team to each league. In 2023, MLB adjusted the schedule so that each MLB team plays each of the 29 other teams at least once during the regular season.

TIMELINE

1903

MLB begins

1921

A single commissioner is chosen to lead MLB

1922

The World Series is shifted to a seven-game format

7

1947

Jackie Robinson is the first Black player in MLB

1961

MLB begins to expand

1977

Two more AL teams are added to MLB

1993

Two more NL teams are added to MLB

1997

Interleague play begins

1998

The AL and NL each add a team, bringing the total number of MLB teams to 30

2013

The Houston Astros move from the NL to the AL to make two 15-team leagues

2022

The NL adopts the designated hitter rule

TWO TEAMS IN A CITY

Three U.S. cities have two MLB teams. New York, Los Angeles, and Chicago are home to both an AL and NL team.

TERRIFIC TEAMS

1927 NEW YORK YANKEES

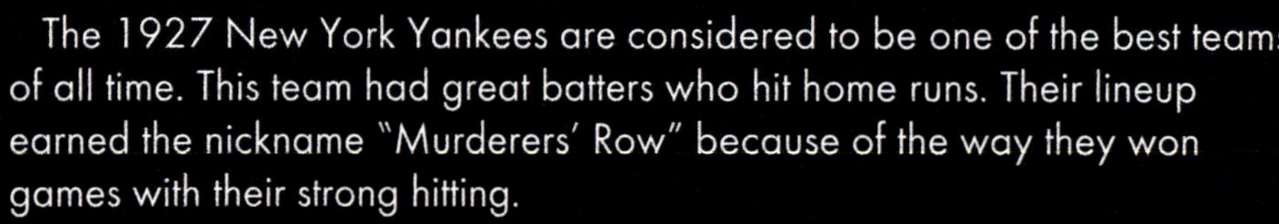

The 1927 New York Yankees are considered to be one of the best teams of all time. This team had great batters who hit home runs. Their lineup earned the nickname "Murderers' Row" because of the way they won games with their strong hitting.

Babe Ruth hit 60 home runs that year. This was the single season record for home runs at the time. He hit more home runs by himself than any other AL team did that year. His teammate Lou Gehrig hit 47. Bob Meusel, Earle Combs, and Tony Lazzeri were other strong hitters on the team. The Yankees also had the best pitchers in MLB.

The Yankees started the season with strong wins over the Philadelphia Athletics. The Yankees were first place in the AL from the beginning of the season to the end. They won 110 games and finished the season 19 games ahead of the second-place Athletics. The Yankees faced the Pittsburgh Pirates in the World Series. They **swept** the Pirates in four games and nailed down their reputation as one of the all-time great teams.

SUPER STAR
LOU GEHRIG
POSITION
FIRST BASEMAN
KEY STAT
173 RUNS BATTED IN
BABE RUTH
1927 RECORD
REGULAR SEASON
110—44—1
WIN LOSS TIE
WORLD SERIES
4—0
WIN LOSS

1929 PHILADELPHIA ATHLETICS

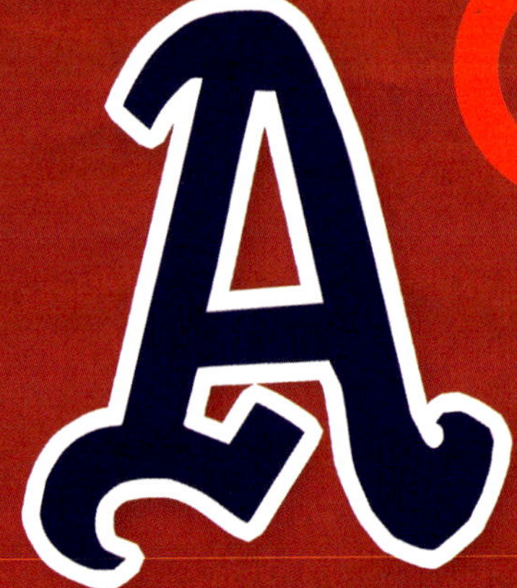

The Philadelphia Athletics, or the A's, were baseball's best team in 1929. Baseball historians call them one of the all-time great teams. The A's finished second to the Yankees in the AL in 1927 and 1928. But in 1929, the A's had the best record in the AL, beating the Yankees by 18 games. A's pitcher Lefty Grove led the league with 170 strikeouts. Mickey Cochrane, Jimmie Foxx, and Al Simmons were their three strongest hitters. Cochrane's **batting average** was .331, while Foxx batted .354 and Simmons batted .365. Foxx hit 33 home runs that year and Simmons hit 34.

In the World Series, the A's faced the Chicago Cubs. The A's won the first two games. Then the Cubs won the third game. In the fourth game, it looked like the Cubs might win again. In the seventh inning, the Cubs were ahead 8-0. Fans started to leave, thinking the Cubs had won. But the A's began to get hits and score runs. The A's kept scoring, winning the game 10-8. They **clinched** the World Series in the fifth game with a 3-2 win over the Cubs.

WINNING STREAK

The Athletics kept winning after 1929. They won the World Series again in 1930. In 1931 they won the AL again, but lost in the World Series.

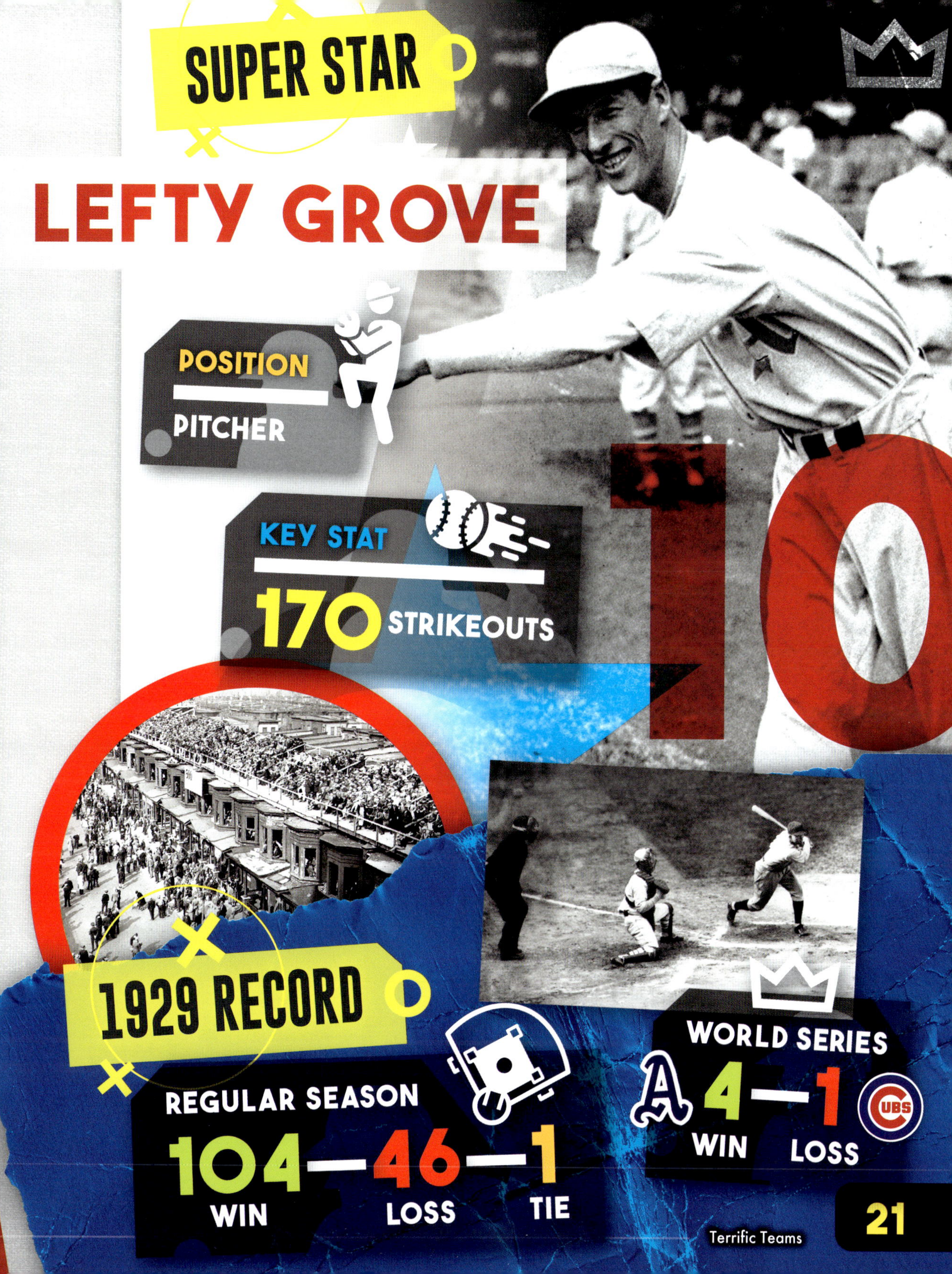
SUPER STAR
LEFTY GROVE
POSITION
PITCHER
KEY STAT
170 STRIKEOUTS
10
1929 RECORD
REGULAR SEASON
104—46—1
WIN LOSS TIE
WORLD SERIES
A 4—1 CUBS
WIN LOSS

1970 BALTIMORE ORIOLES

The 1970 Baltimore Orioles were packed with powerful pitchers. Dave McNally, Mike Cuellar, and Jim Palmer all won 20 games or more. The Orioles finished the season as the best team in the AL. They won their division by 15 games. Frank Robinson and Boog Powell were the team's top hitters. Robinson, the right fielder, batted .306. Powell, the first baseman, hit 35 home runs with 114 runs-batted-in. The Orioles had a strong defense too. Brooks Robinson, Davey Johnson, and Paul Blair all won Gold Glove awards in that season.

MIKE CUELLAR

In the AL Championship Series, the Orioles beat the Minnesota Twins in three straight games. The Orioles then moved on to the World Series. In 1969, they had lost the World Series to the New York Mets. In 1970, they faced a strong Cincinnati Reds team. The Orioles took the first three games of the series. But the Reds won a close Game 4. In the fifth game, the Orioles came back to win after being down 3-0 early in the game. Third baseman Brooks Robinson finished the series with a .429 batting average and was named the World Series MVP.

1970 WORLD SERIES

1970 RECORD

REGULAR SEASON

AL CHAMPIONSHIP SERIES

WORLD SERIES

SUPER STAR

BROOKS ROBINSON

POSITION

THIRD BASEMAN

KEY STAT

1970 GOLD GLOVE WINNER

1976 CINCINNATI REDS

In 1975, the Cincinnati Reds won the World Series. In 1976, they came back even stronger. The 1976 Reds were called the "Big Red Machine." Their starting lineup was called "the Great Eight." It included Johnny Bench at catcher, Tony Pérez at first base, Joe Morgan at second base, Dave Concepción at shortstop, and Pete Rose at third base. Ken Griffey, César Gerónimo, and George Foster played in the outfield.

The Reds won 102 games in the regular season. It truly was a team effort. Six of the Great Eight players had season batting averages of .280 or higher. The team's pitching was strong too. Manager Sparky Anderson swapped other players into the Great Eight lineup throughout the season. But when they reached the postseason, the Great Eight played all the playoff and World Series games.

In the postseason, the Reds did not lose a game. Catcher Johnny Bench batted .444 in the postseason and hit three home runs. The Reds defeated the Philadelphia Phillies in three games to win the NL Championship Series. Then, they beat the New York Yankees in four straight games to become back-to-back World Series champions!

TONY PÉREZ

SUPER STAR

JOHNNY BENCH

POSITION

CATCHER

KEN GRIFFEY IN THE 1976 WORLD SERIES

KEY STAT

.444 POSTSEASON BATTING AVERAGE

NL CHAMPIONSHIP SERIES

3 WIN — 0 LOSS

1976 RECORD

REGULAR SEASON

102 WIN — 60 LOSS — 0 TIE

WORLD SERIES

4 WIN — 0 LOSS

MLB GREATS

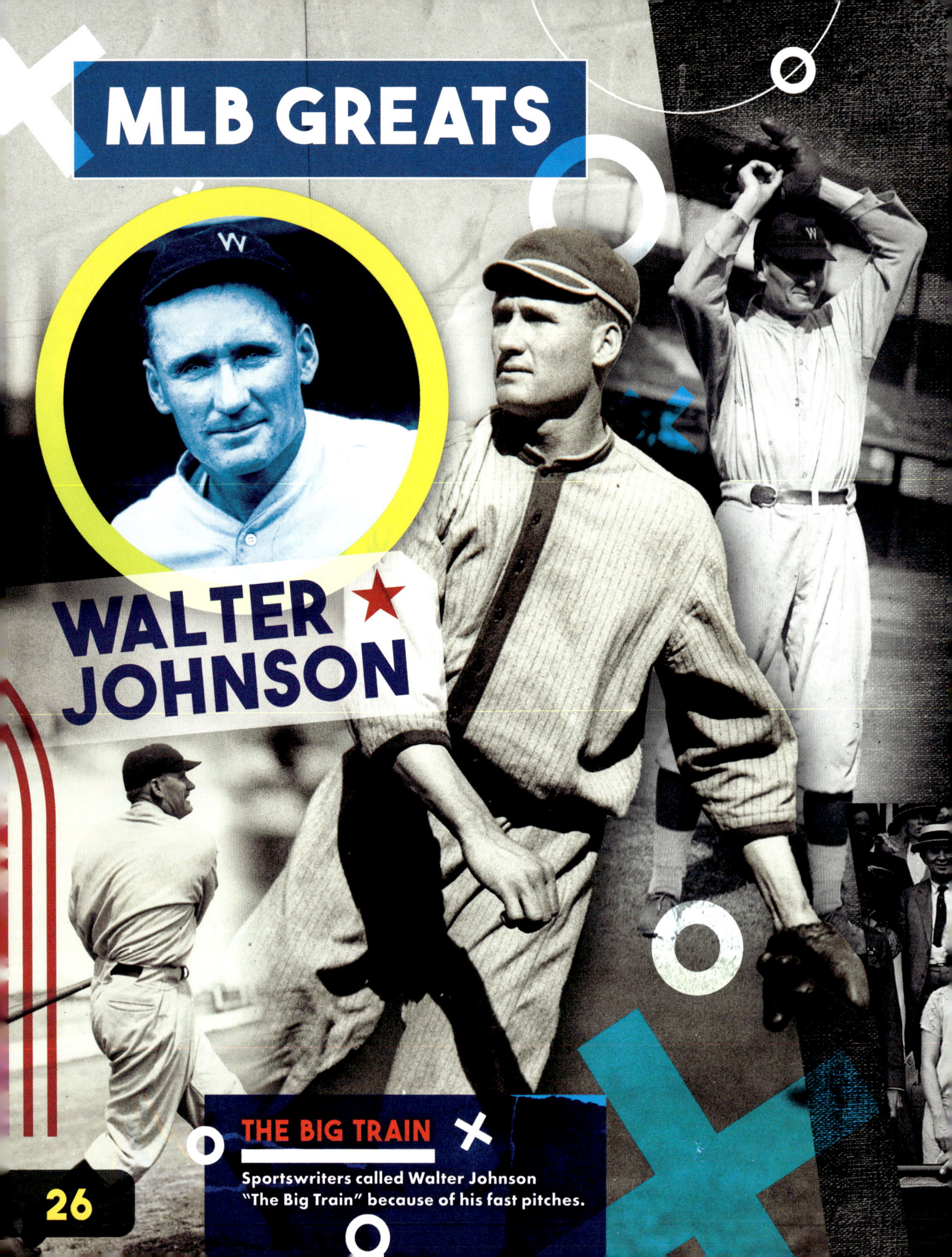

WALTER JOHNSON

THE BIG TRAIN

Sportswriters called Walter Johnson "The Big Train" because of his fast pitches.

Walter Johnson was a right-handed pitcher with a powerful fastball. Johnson pitched for the Washington Senators from 1907 to 1927. He first played baseball at age 16. Coaches soon noticed his strong fastball. Right after high school he joined a **semipro** team in Idaho. By age 19 he was pitching in Washington, D.C., for the Washington Senators.

The Senators were not a very good team when Johnson arrived. They had never finished better than sixth place in the AL. Over time, the Senators' record improved. Johnson's great pitching is credited with playing an important role in their rise in the standings. In 1924, the Senators won the AL. They played the New York Giants in the World Series. In Game 7, Johnson threw four shutout innings to close the game. The Senators won the World Series with Johnson as the winning pitcher. Johnson played for the Senators for 21 seasons with an amazing pitching record. He won 417 games. In 11 seasons his **earned run average** was below 2.00. Johnson struck out 3,509 batters during his career. This was a record for strikeouts that stood for over 50 years. He holds the career record for shutouts with 110.

PROFILE

HEIGHT 6 FT 1 IN

BIRTHDAY NOVEMBER 6, 1887

POSITION PITCHER

YEAR SIGNED 1907

YEARS ACTIVE 1907–1927

TEAM W WASHINGTON SENATORS

AWARDS & RECORDS

417 WINS

110 SHUTOUTS

3,509 STRIKEOUTS

531 COMPLETE GAMES

1936 ELECTED TO HALL OF FAME

2 TIME MVP

George Herman Ruth, Jr., was famous for hitting home runs. As a teenager, he played baseball for a minor league team. Sportswriters soon gave him the nickname Babe. During the 1914 season, Ruth moved up to the majors, playing for the Boston Red Sox. Ruth was a pitcher and outfielder. In 1920, he was traded to the New York Yankees.

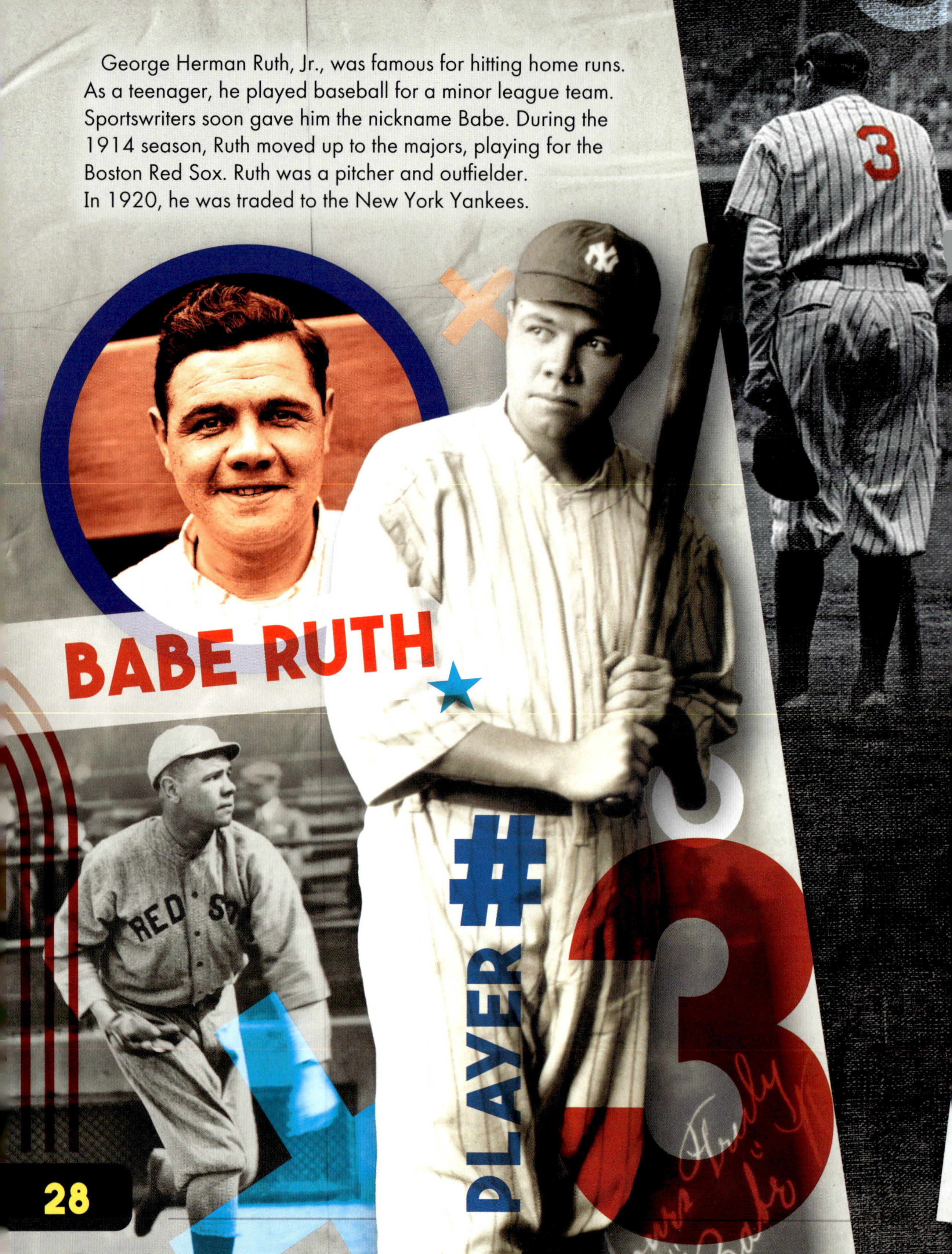

Ruth's greatest success came playing for the Yankees. He hit so many home runs that sportswriters called him the "Sultan of Swat" and called Yankee Stadium "The House That Ruth Built." In 1927, Ruth hit a single-season record 60 home runs. That record would not be broken until Roger Maris hit 61 home runs in 1961. During his years playing with the Yankees, Ruth helped the team win four World Series. In 1935, Ruth left the Yankees to play his last season for the Boston Braves. Ruth hit 714 home runs during his career.

Ruth's home run hitting changed the game of baseball. Because of his hitting power, baseball became a more **offensive** game, with a focus on home runs and runs scored. Sportswriters and fans alike loved him and the excitement he brought to the game.

HEIGHT 6 FT 2 IN

BIRTHDAY FEBRUARY 6, 1895

POSITIONS OUTFIELDER, PITCHER

YEAR SIGNED 1914

YEARS ACTIVE 1914–1935

TEAMS

BOSTON RED SOX

NEW YORK YANKEES

BOSTON BRAVES

AWARDS & RECORDS

714 HOME RUNS

2,214 RUNS BATTED IN

WILLIE MAYS

Willie Mays was one of the best all-around players of all time. Mays came from a baseball family. Both his father and grandfather played baseball. While he was still in high school, Mays joined the Birmingham Black Barons. This team played in a **Negro League**. Mays only played in the Sunday games while he was still attending classes. After high school in 1950, he signed a contract with the New York Giants and joined their minor league team. In 1951, Mays was called up to the major league team. He played well and was named the NL Rookie of the Year.

In 1952, Mays left baseball to serve in the Army. He returned to the Giants for the 1954 season. That year, the Giants won the NL title and the World Series. Mays was named the NL MVP in 1954 and again in 1965. He played for the Giants for 21 seasons. During his years with the Giants, he won a Gold Glove in 12 consecutive seasons. He played his last two seasons in MLB with the New York Mets before he retired in 1973. Mays finished his career with 3,293 hits and 660 home runs.

BIRTHDAY MAY 6, 1931

POSITION CENTER FIELDER

YEAR SIGNED 1950

YEARS ACTIVE 1951–1952, 1954–1973

TEAMS

NEW YORK GIANTS

SAN FRANCISCO GIANTS

NEW YORK METS

AWARDS & RECORDS

3,293 HITS

10,924 AT BATS

12 GOLD GLOVE AWARDS

.301 LIFETIME BATTING AVERAGE

1979 ELECTED TO HALL OF FAME

2 TIME MVP

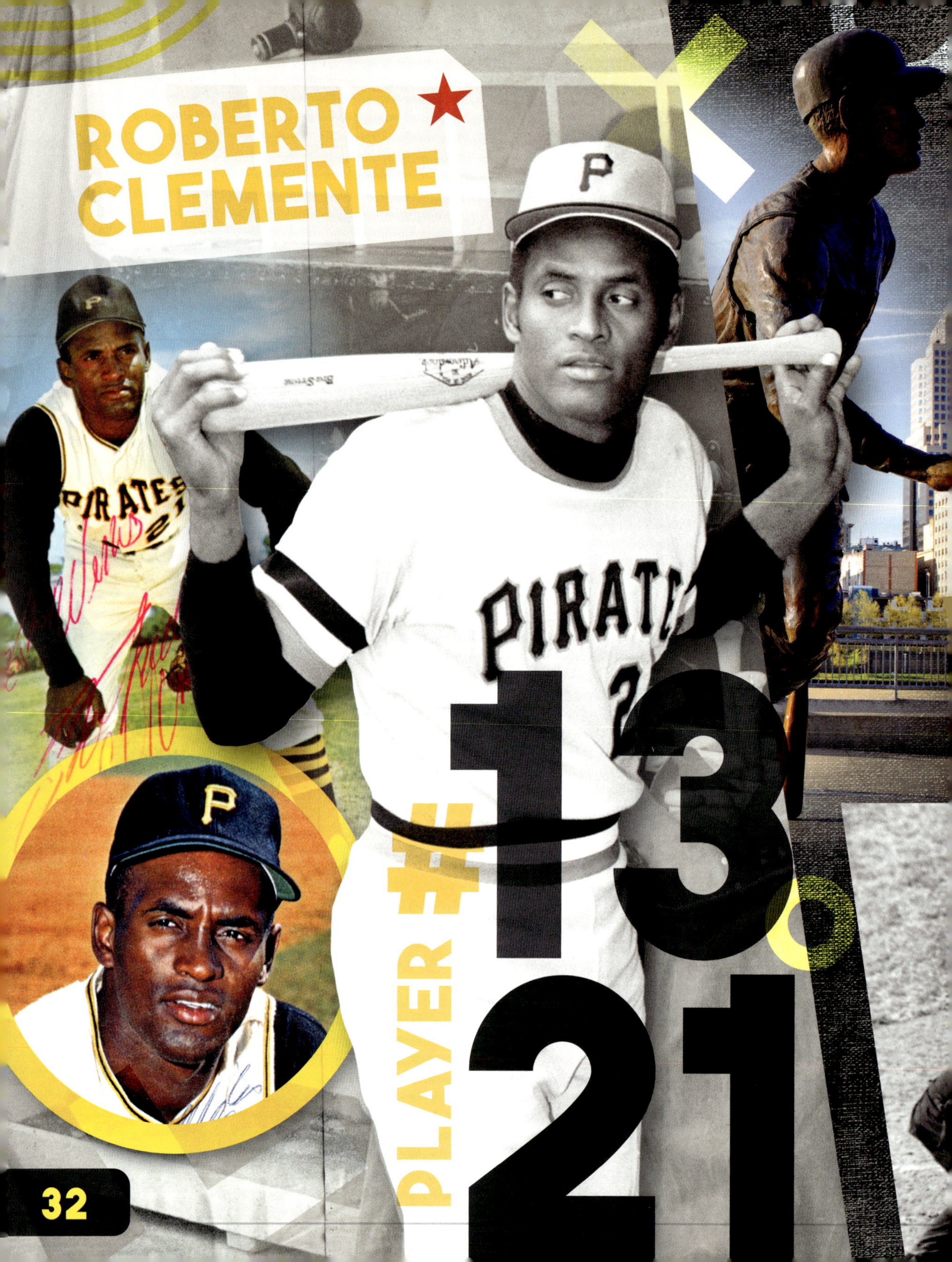
ROBERTO CLEMENTE
PLAYER #13
21
PIRATES

Roberto Clemente was born in Puerto Rico. At age 17, he joined a team in the Puerto Rican Baseball League. In 1954, the Brooklyn Dodgers signed him to play with their minor league team. In 1955, he joined the Pittsburgh Pirates and began playing major league ball. He became known for his throwing and running skills. Clemente became the first Latin American player to get 3,000 hits. He won 12 Gold Glove awards and four NL batting titles. Clemente was named the NL MVP in 1966. His strong hitting helped the Pirates win the 1960 and 1971 World Series. Clemente was named the World Series MVP in 1971.

In December 1972, an earthquake hit Nicaragua. Clemente guided relief efforts to send aid from Puerto Rico. On December 31, he traveled on a plane carrying relief supplies from Puerto Rico to Nicaragua. The plane crashed, and Clemente passed away. In 1973, Clemente was added to the Hall of Fame. He was the first player born in Latin America to be added. The same year, MLB renamed their award for excellent sportsmanship and community service to the Roberto Clemente Award.

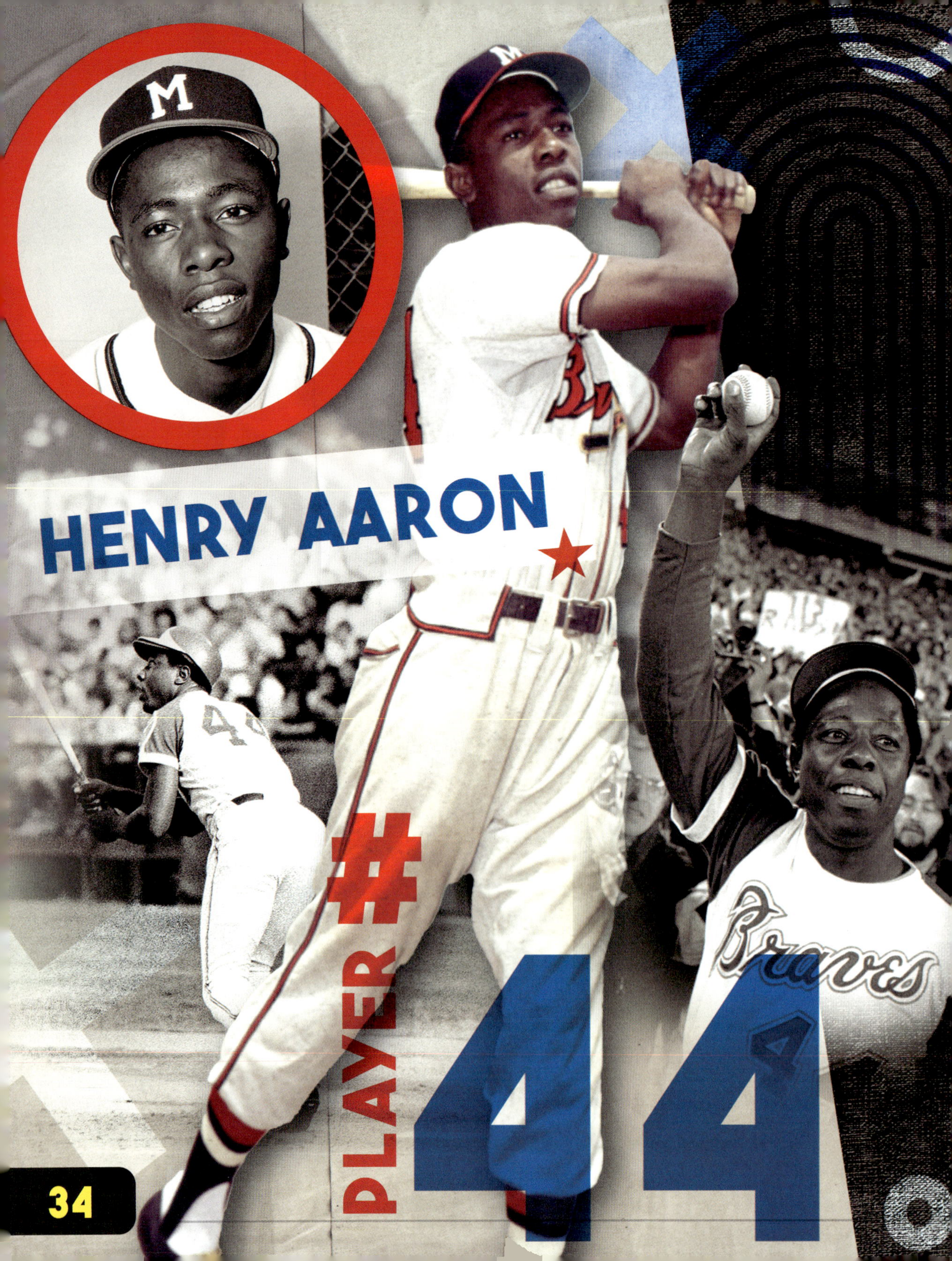
HENRY AARON
PLAYER #44
Braves

Henry Aaron was known for his hitting. It earned him the nickname "Hammerin' Hank." Aaron started his baseball career in 1952 at age 18 playing for the Indianapolis Clowns of the Negro American League. Later that same year, he signed with the Boston Braves. In 1954, he reached the major leagues. The Braves had moved to Milwaukee and become the Milwaukee Braves. In 1957, Aaron helped the Braves win the World Series. He was also named the NL MVP.

When the Braves moved to Atlanta in 1966, Aaron was on his way to breaking Babe Ruth's career home run record. He broke the record in 1974 when he hit his 715th home run. At the end of the 1974 season, the Braves traded Aaron to the Milwaukee Brewers. He retired at the end of the 1976 season. Aaron hit 755 home runs during his career. He holds the MLB record for runs batted in with 2,297. Aaron was not just a hitter. He was an excellent fielder, too. He won three Gold Glove awards and was chosen to play in the All-Star Game 25 times. Aaron was elected to the Hall of Fame in 1982.

ATLANTA BRAVES

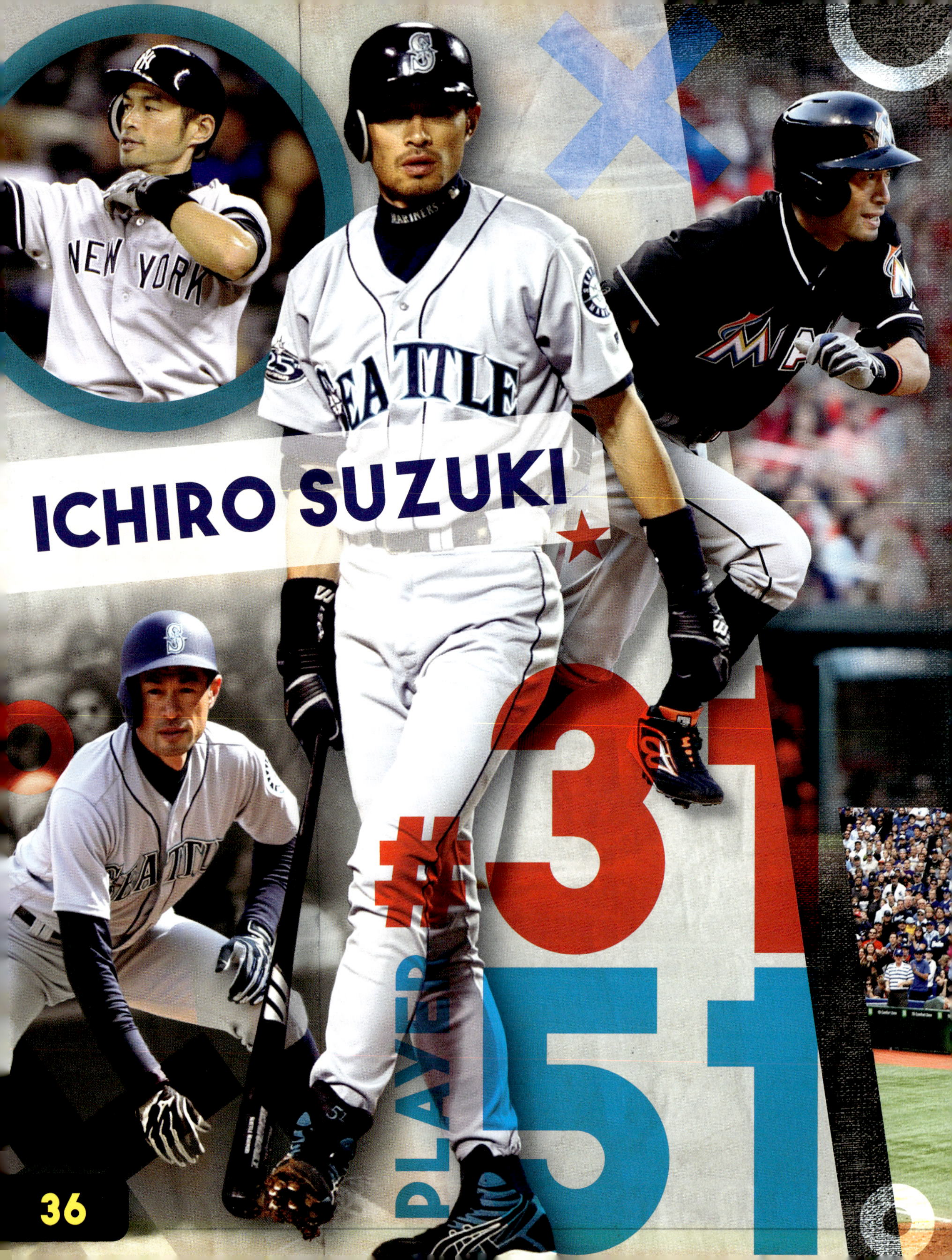
ICHIRO SUZUKI
#31
PLAYER
51

Ichiro Suzuki started his baseball career in Japan in 1992. He won the Japanese batting title and a Gold Glove award seven years in a row. In 2001, the Seattle Mariners signed Suzuki. Many people thought Suzuki might struggle hitting against MLB pitchers. They were wrong. Suzuki was named the AL Rookie of the Year and AL MVP in his first season with the Mariners. His .350 batting average was the highest in the league. He also led the league with 56 stolen bases. In 2004, he won the AL batting title again with a .372 average. In his first 10 years in the league, he won 10 straight Gold Gloves. He was also named to 10 straight All-Star Games.

In 2012, the Mariners traded Suzuki to the New York Yankees. In 2015, he joined the Miami Marlins. He returned to Seattle in 2018. When his career ended in 2019, Suzuki had 3,089 hits. Along with the 1,278 hits he got playing in Japan, Suzuki became the pro baseball player with the most total hits. Suzuki was the first Japanese position player to have great success playing with MLB teams. Stars like Hideki Matsui and Shohei Ohtani would follow in his footsteps.

TEAMS

SEATTLE MARINERS

NEW YORK YANKEES

MIAMI MARLINS

AWARDS & RECORDS

117 HOME RUNS

1,420 RUNS

3,089 HITS

9,934 AT BATS

10 GOLD GLOVE AWARDS

.311 LIFETIME BATTING AVERAGE

2025 ELECTED TO HALL OF FAME

509 STOLEN BASES

1 TIME MVP

MEMORABLE MOMENTS

BABE RUTH CALLS HIS SHOT

In the 1932 World Series, the New York Yankees faced the Chicago Cubs. The Yankees won the first two games in New York. Game 3 was played in Chicago. Chicago fans showed up to support their Cubs and booed the Yankees with great enthusiasm.

In the bottom of the fourth inning, the score was tied 4–4. With one out in the top of the fifth inning, Ruth came to bat. Players on the Cubs bench were taunting him as he walked out to home plate. Ruth was yelling back at the Cubs. Charlie Root, the Cubs pitcher, soon had two balls and two strikes on Ruth. Then Ruth paused and pointed his right hand toward center field. Ruth hit the next pitch over the center field wall and into the seats. Home run! The pitcher said later that Ruth was just pointing two fingers, showing that he had two strikes with one strike left. But newspaper stories the next day reported that Ruth had called his home run, and the story stuck. The Yankees went on to win the game, and the next day they won the World Series.

WRIGLEY FIELD
4
NEW YORK

JACKIE ROBINSON BREAKS THE "COLOR LINE" IN BASEBALL

1932 NEGRO LEAGUE ALL-STAR TEAM

In the early 1900s, MLB was **segregated**. White players played on MLB teams. Black players played in the Negro Leagues. The Black players were as talented as white players. But people's **prejudices** and **Jim Crow laws** prevented Black players from playing on the same teams as white players.

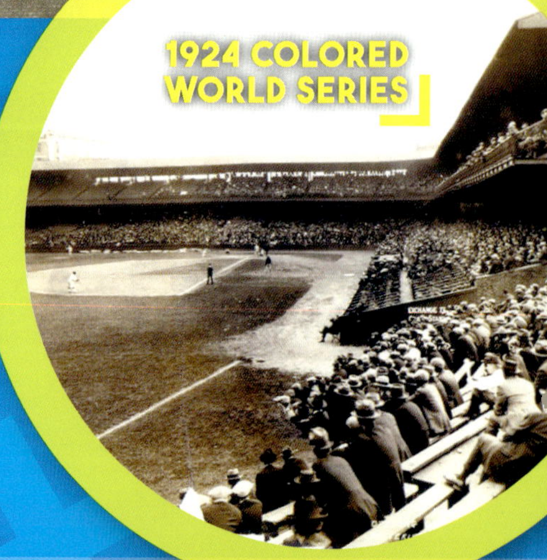

1924 COLORED WORLD SERIES

Change came on April 15, 1947, when a Black player named Jackie Robinson played his first game for the Brooklyn Dodgers. Before coming to the Dodgers, Robinson played with the Kansas City Monarchs in the Negro American League. Some fans and players opposed Robinson playing for the Dodgers. He was treated harshly. Jim Crow laws kept him from staying in the same hotels and eating in the same restaurants as his white teammates. But Robinson did not quit.

Robinson quieted some of the criticism with his baseball talents. He was named Rookie of the Year in 1947. In 1949, he won the NL batting championship and was voted NL MVP. Robinson entered the Hall of Fame in 1962. He was the first Black person to be honored in this way.

JACKIE ROBINSON

JACKIE ROBINSON DAY

Every year on April 15, MLB celebrates Jackie Robinson Day. On that day, every player in the league wears Robinson's number 42 to honor his accomplishments.

KIRBY PUCKETT'S WALK-OFF HOME RUN

KIRBY PUCKETT

In the 1991 World Series, the Minnesota Twins faced the Atlanta Braves. Both teams had finished last place in their division the previous year. In the World Series, both teams played tight games. Three of the first five games of the series were decided by only one run. By Game 6, the Braves led the Twins three games to two.

In Game 6, the Twins scored first. In the third inning, Twins center fielder Kirby Puckett made a spectacular catch in left-center field, preventing an extra-base hit for the Braves. In the fifth inning, the Braves tied the score 2–2. But Puckett quickly hit a home run to move the Twins ahead again 3–2. In the seventh inning, the Braves tied the game again. The game stayed tied 3–3 until the bottom of the 11th inning. Puckett came to bat, facing pitcher Charlie Leibrandt. Puckett swung at a high pitch. The ball flew over the left-center field wall. A walk-off home run! The Twins win brought the series to a Game 7 to decide the champion. The Twins won Game 7 with a score of 1–0. They were the 1991 World Series champs!

TWINS CELEBRATE
AFTER WINNING
GAME 6

MLB BY THE NUMBERS

MLB WAS FOUNDED IN 1903.
THE FIRST MLB GAME WAS PLAYED ON APRIL 16, 1903.

OLDEST TEAMS
FOUNDED 1871
ATLANTA BRAVES
CHICAGO CUBS
ICHIRO SUZUKI
MOST SINGLE-SEASON HITS
262
HITS IN 2004
MOST CAREER STRIKEOUTS
5,714
BATTERS
NOLAN RYAN
LARGEST STADIUM
DODGERS STADIUM, LOS ANGELES, CALIFORNIA
56,000
PEOPLE
MOST WORLD SERIES TITLES
AS OF 2024
27
TITLES
MOST CAREER STEALS
1,406
BASES
RICKEY HENDERSON

GLOSSARY

American League—one of the two major leagues that make up MLB; the other is the National League.

batting average—a number determined by dividing a player's hits by their total at-bats

clinched—won enough that there was no possibility for another team to win

commissioner—a person in charge of a sports league

consecutive—in a row

divisions—groups of teams that often play each other

draft—a process during which professional teams choose high school and college athletes to play for them

earned run average—a number that measures how many earned runs a pitcher allows per nine innings pitched; earned runs are runs that are scored without errors.

farm system—minor league teams that belong to an MLB team whose players eventually play for the MLB team

interleague—related to regular-season games where an AL team plays an NL team

Jim Crow laws—United States laws that enforced racial segregation from the late 1870s until the 1960s

minor league—related to professional baseball leagues below Major League Baseball

National League—one of the two major leagues in the MLB; the other is the American League.

Negro League—one of many former leagues of professional baseball teams made up of only Black players

offensive—related to players who are trying to score

playoff—related to games played after the regular season is over; playoff games determine which teams play in the championship game.

postseason—games played after the regular season

prejudices—negative opinions formed without any knowledge or experience

preseason—games played before the regular season; preseason games do not count toward a team's record.

segregated—separated based on race

semipro—related to teams that make money for playing, but not enough that it is their main job; semipro stands for semiprofessional.

swept—won a series of games without any losses

walk-off—related to a hit that ends a game

Wild Card—related to teams that reach the postseason even though they do not win their division

WRITE ABOUT IT!

- Who do you think is the greatest baseball player of all time and **why?**

- Which moment in MLB's history do you think is the most important and **why?**

- Which of baseball's greatest teams do you think was the best? Do you think that team would still be the best team playing today?

ALSO CHECK OUT

INDEX

The images in this book are reproduced through the courtesy of: ASSOCIATED PRESS/ AP Images, front cover, pp. 1, 3 (Suzuki), 8 (Spring, Cy Young), 9 (draft), 10 (Hall of Fame, Playoffs), 14 (top, bottom), 20 (all), 21 (all), 22 (all), 24 (all), 25 (all), 30 (main, right), 32 (main), 33, 34 (all), 35, 36 (Suzuki, inset), 39 (field), 41, 42 (top, bottom), 43 (all), 46 (main), 48 (main); Boston Public Library/ Wikimedia Commons, front cover, pp. 1, 12 (fun fact); Mobilus In Mobili/ Wikimedia Commons, front cover, p. 1; Erik Drost/ Wikimedia Commons, front cover, pp. 1, 11 (trophy), 45 (trophy); Heritage Auctions/ Wikimedia Commons, pp. 2, 3 (Mays), 19 (Gehrig), 26, 30 (Mays); Library of Congress/ Wikimedia Commons, pp. 3 (Ruth), 19 (Ruth), 26 (right), 27, 28 (Ruth); Daniel Shirey/ Getty Images, pp. 4 (all), 10 (World Series); Cooper Neill/ Getty Images, p. 5 (field); Rob Tringali/ Getty Images, p. 5 (home run, bottom); Sipa USA/ Alamy Stock Photo, p. 6 (bottom); PA Images/ Alamy Stock Photo, p. 6 (top); Tim Davis/ Alamy Stock Photo, p. 7; Image of sport/ Alamy Stock Photo, p. 8 (top); Robert Taylor/ Wikimedia Commons, p. 8 (Cy Young inset); UPI/ Alamy Stock Photo, p. 9 (golden glove); oaktree_brian_1976/ Wikimedia Commons, p. 9 (golden glove inset); Mary DeCicco/ Getty Images, p. 9 (MVP); Thomson200/ Wikimedia Commons, p. 9 (MVP inset); Hum Images/ Alamy Stock Photo, p. 12; Nathaniel Currier/ Alamy Stock Photo, p. 13 (top); National Baseball Hall of Fame Library/ Wikimedia Commons, p. 13 (bottom); Alon Alexander/ Alamy Stock Photo, p. 14 (middle); Rich Pilling/ Getty Images, p. 15; Sea Cow/ Wikimedia Commons, p. 15 (fun fact); Otto Greule Jr/ Getty Images, p. 16 (top); Tribune Content Agency LLC/ Alamy Stock Photo, pp. 16 (bottom), 36 (right); Unknown/ Wikimedia Commons, pp. 17 (1921), 18, 39 (bottom), 40 (inset); Focus On Sport/ Getty Images, pp. 17 (1977), 23; Stephen Dunn/ Getty Images, p. 17 (1993); Tom Hagerty/ Wikimedia Commons, p. 17 (2013); Iuliia Sokolovska, p. 17 (fun fact); Underwood & Underwood/ Wikimedia Commons, p. 19; Jackson, William Henry/ Wikimedia Commons, p. 26 (inset); International News/ Wikimedia Commons, p. 26 (left); Heritage Auction Gallery/ Wikimedia Commons, p. 28 (inset); Francis P. Burke/ Wikimedia Commons, p. 28 (left); New York Herald Tribune/ Wikimedia Commons, p. 28 (right); Goudey/ Wikimedia Commons, p. 29; William C. Greene/ Wikimedia Commons, p. 30 (inset); Underwood Archives, Inc/ Alamy Stock Photo, p. 31; RLFE Pix/ Alamy Stock Photo, pp. 32 (inset, left), 45 (Ryan); kirkikis, pp. 32 (right), 45 (background); Andy Witchger/ Wikimedia Commons, p. 36 (left); James G/ Wikimedia Commons, p. 37; Transcendental Graphics/ Getty Images, p. 38; B Bennett/ Getty Images, p. 39 (top); RMY Auctions/ Wikimedia Commons, p. 40; National Portrait Gallery/ Wikimedia Commons, p. 41 (Robinson); John Iacono/ Getty Images, p. 42 (middle); Jim Accordino/ Wikimedia Commons, p. 44 (Bonds); Mears Auctions/ Wikimedia Commons, p. 44 (Young); Jeffrey Hayes/ Wikimedia Commons, p. 45 (Suzuki); Kit Leong, p. 45 (stadium); Zuma Press, Inc./ Alamy Stock Photo, p. 45 (Henderson).